Waiting for the Sunrise

Waiting for the Sunrise

Poems
Barbara Berkenfield

Drawings
Susan Berkenfield

SUNSTONE
PRESS

SANTA FE

Other Books by Barbara Berkenfield

Driving Toward the Moon, 2005
The Earth Behind My Thumb, 2008
Turning to the Sunset, 2011

Sunstone books may be purchased for educational, business, or sales promotional use.
For information please write: Special Markets Department, Sunstone Press,
P.O. Box 2321, Santa Fe, New Mexico 87504-2321.

Book and Cover design › Vicki Ahl
Body typeface › Bell
Printed on acid-free paper
∞
eBook 978-1-61139-280-7

Library of Congress Cataloging-in-Publication Data

Berkenfield, Barbara, 1935-
[Poems. Selections]
Waiting for the sunrise : poems / by Barbara Berkenfield ;
drawings by Susan Berkenfield.
    pages ; cm
ISBN 978-0-86534-992-6 (softcover : alk. paper)
I. Title.
PS3602.E7566A6 2014
811'.6--dc23
                                2014013930

WWW.SUNSTONEPRESS.COM
SUNSTONE PRESS / POST OFFICE BOX 2321 / SANTA FE, NM 87504-2321 /USA
(505) 988-4418 / ORDERS ONLY (800) 243-5644 / FAX (505) 988-1025

This book is dedicated to
all creative spirits who bring
beauty to our world.

CONTENTS

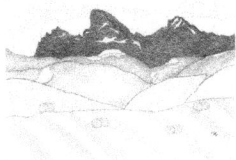

HISTORY LESSONS

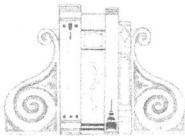

FAMILY AND FRIENDS

CODA

LANDSCAPE

The Sleeping Ute

Blanketed by snow
Or dry from summer heat,
He stretches for miles
Along the earth.

A stone giant
Sleeping on his back,
Facing skyward,
Offering prayers
To the heavens.

The eagles soar upward
Carrying his messages
To the gods.

On a road in Utah's Four Corners area, October 2011

The Messenger

The wind blew
Wild and gusting,
Background music
In my restless sleep.

When morning came
I walked through
Flecks of ash
White, grey and black
And found a single leaf.

In the morning stillness,
Curled and fragile,
Carbon black
It lay resting
On the street.

Carefully I placed it
In my hand
Noting the tiny veins
And curving outline
Of a mountain oak.

This blackened messenger
Had traveled with the wind
From the mountains
Thirty miles away,
Heralding the dangers
Of a raging fire.

Fire in the Jemez Mountains, June 2011

Linemen

Single file
To the horizon
Long-legged giants,
Stick figures
Whose short arms
Carry the lines
Bringing power
To all the West.

Shouldn't we thank them,
These stilted monsters
Who transmit our burdens
In summer heat
And winter snow?
Without complaint
They march,
Impervious to all
But the lightning bolts
Hurled from dark heavens.

Along a Wyoming highway, September 2011

Rain Today

When it began
We rushed inside
And stood
Counting rain drops
Running down the window.

You would have thought
We had never seen
Rain before.

For months
Only a faint memory,
The smell of wet earth
Was intoxicating.

Garden colors brightened.
Worries eased
As cool air
Filled the house
To banish record heat
Trapped inside our walls.

It was not soon enough
To relieve our Western world
Consumed by drought, wind, and fire.

But, as it drummed the roof,
We sighed as one,
Becoming hopeful
That at least this summer,
We would be spared.

A summer party, 2012

Grass

Three years of drought,
The palette of my world
Has shrunk to blue and brown.

Bright blue skies
With passing clouds
Give rose and purple sunsets
Or unfulfilled promises of rain.

At my feet a desert-scape
Of bare, brown earth,
Hard-packed like clay,
Stretches from house to house.
Strong spring winds
Make the surface
Dance with devil dust.

This summer
Clouds gather,
Stack high above me
Bringing gentle, female rains.

Once again
Our days
Are carpeted in
Shades of green.

Grasses and welcome weeds
Blend together
In a green sea
To the horizon.

What miracle
Can keep their seeds,
Hidden for years,
Sprout and grow each day?
It is a wonder unexplained.

Santa Fe Summer 2013

Fields of Flowers

Trash and broken glass
Transformed to molten seas,
Crannies of our town,
From weed-choked empty lots
To small dirt corner islands,
Are spread with golden carpets.

The flowers musty perfume
Permeates the air.
Littered roadsides
Now edged in yellow ribbons.

September rains
Have made our world,
Dazzling in the afternoon sun,
Unlike any autumn
We can recall.

Autumn, 2013

WILD AND TAME

Ode to a Prairie Dog

We never met until today
When to Prairie Heaven
I sent you on your way.

You ran in front.
I could not stop.
I tried to swerve,
But in your fright
You turned around
For Prairie Town.

A thud and bump,
Hit and run,
And suddenly
Your day was done.

I'm sorry as one can be
And hope some day
You'll pardon me.

On the road, June 2011

Messages in the Grass

Dogs smell thousands
Of seductive scents
With each inhalation.

No wonder Beau
Devotes endless moments
To a single blade
Of tall, dry grass,
Nature's form of Facebook.

Think of all the messages
He is receiving
From creatures large and small
Touching it as they passed.

How his nose twitches
And drops of moisture form.
How long does each message last
Along one blade of grass?

Rooted, there he stays,
Leaving his own reply
Until my patience fades
And I assert control.

We continue our morning stroll
Only to stop again
Where the next messages prevail.

Spring walk, May 2013

Osprey

Last month,
Fast she fell
From the sky,
Buckshot in the chest.

Retrieved and healed,
Now time for release
Back to her world.

They reach to free her
From the cage
Blanketed and hooded
For protection.

Our son's hands
Wrap around her wings
And hold her close.
Her strong talons hang still.
Tail feathers sheathed in plastic
Are gently freed.

Her strength against his chest,
She is un-hooded now
And set down upon the bank
To rest in high grass
Above the summer-slow river.

Eyes focused,
Her wings stretch back,
Open stiffly.
Unsteadily she rises.
Flying low, she turns away.

With awkward wings
Stuttering
She drops into the sage.

We rise as one,
Turn to watch her
Fly once more.
Slowly her wings remember flight
And she gains height.
More smoothly now
She heads toward the hills.

High above us
Another soars the draft in circles
Clutching a fish
And screaming
"Stay away, this space is mine."

We look back
To the now-small speck
Flying far from us.
Silently, we send our prayers
To her for courage and long life.

By the Teton River, Summer 2013

The Nest

Beau leads the way
As we head across the empty lot,
Eroding more of a path
Already worn to dusty grooves
As it winds between the cacti.

He stops to poke muzzle
Inside a cholla's wicked branches
Armed with thorns.

I am surprised
That my high desert dog,
Who learned long ago
To shun their embrace,
Is so entranced today.

Then find a tiny nest
Concealed deep within.
With three green jewels
Secreted from predators
By protective parents.

In spite of the thorny armor
Shielding them,
I am uneasy.
This small womb
Is too close to the ground.

We stop by each day,
Relieved to find them safe.
But today the nest was tilted.
The green eggs gone,

Perhaps a morsel
For beast, snake or bird.

I whisper to the finches
Circling near,
Crying shrill in mourning,
I told you so.
I too am bereft.

High desert walk, 2013

The Unicorn

Down the hill
I sought quiet
In a secluded glade
Away from the
Joyful music, dance
And jousting
Of Renaissance Fair.

There I saw
A grand white horse,
Still as porcelain
Under the cottonwood's
Dappled shade.
A single horn
Nestled between
His upright ears.

His unearthly rider,
A vision all in white.
Her flowing skirt
Spread across his back.
This fairy princess
Caressed his mane,
Her butterfly wings
Fluttering in the breeze.

A crowd of children,
Completely hushed,
Entranced by this amazing steed,
Circled round
To touch his sides.
No sound except

The rider's soft voice
As she trapped them
In her story's web.

I stepped inside this magic circle
Of peace and beauty,
While this enchanted place
 Restored my childhood.

Renaissance Fair at El Rancho de las Golondrinas,
Santa Fe, September 2013

SEASONS

The Changing Tree

In the meadow
Between the hills,
The changing tree
Stands proud,
Aging in great dignity.

His stark branches,
Bare in the cold
Of wintery winds,
Gather snow
Along their limbs.

He creaks and groans
In spring's thaw.
Bathed by warm rains
And soft breezes,
He stretches upward.

Reddish buds gather
On each twig
Unfolding into leaves
Of gentle greens.
They warm his aging arms
And sap flows inside his veins.

He droops and drowses
In summer's heat,
Until autumn returns
With its crisp nights
Warning of the coming
Edge of winter.

Turning cold and dark
While his leaves depart
And sap settles in his heart,
Patiently the changing tree
Waits again for spring.

October 2011

The River Valley

The autumn stubble
Of dry grasses
Stretches along the valley floor,
Coating the flat ridges
Like Saharan dunes.

These smooth terraces
Marking earlier river channels
Centuries old,
Now flank our sides
As we follow the road west to Ennis.

Today, the river cuts deep into the earth,
Hardly visible across the sun-bleached fields.
Only the tops of trees and bushes
Hint at its path below our line of vision.

This quite valley is home
To the swift-flowing Madison
Ever heading westward,
Unstopped by glistening rocks
Parting the water
Into white plumes and spray.

Guides steer float boats,
With determined fishermen,
Against the wind.
A ceaseless current
Marks the surface with wavelets
Above hidden stones.

Low scrubby trees dot the valley
While the deep river channel
Is edged in lush green grasses,
Reeds, shrubs and wildlife.

Hawks and eagles circle overhead
Or dive toward stacks of dried wheat
Casting dark shadows
In late day sun while awaiting winter.

We would never have found
This peaceful valley world,
Distant from our high desert home,
Without Jim's life path
Bringing us here years ago.

The Madison River Valley, Summer 2012

Cascade

Autumn.
Glorious, shimmering leaves
Bedeck the river cottonwoods.

The clear light
Of crisp October mornings
Dazzles,
As it flickers
Through the canopy
Of trembling leaves.

A cascade of gold and silver.

River walk, Autumn 2012

The Garden

Spring.
May is here again.
April winds are quiet.

Nurseries bulge with blooms.
Their colors beckon,
Recalling past years' pleasures
Digging in dark soil.

But the air is dry.
The sun so high,
And nights so cold.

A few new shoots and leaves
Are sheared away
By thirsty rabbits.

A thrasher's beak
Digs frantically in the dirt,
Searching for insects
Nowhere found this year.

What will the summer bring?

May 2013

Waiting for the Sunrise

A sudden breeze
Cools the summer night,
Waking me
To dawn's pale light.

A touch of blue and hint of rose
Wash across the sky.
Birds chatter, shriek
The coo of doves echoes
Down our chimney.

Suddenly
The whir of wings
As hummers leave
Their snug juniper nests
To attack our feeders.

The mountains,
Now rimmed in golden light,
Hold my sight
As I lie in bed
Wondering what the day may bring,
While waiting for the sunrise.

At home, Summer 2013

Summer Walk

A peaceful afternoon
I walk their country road.
Windswept grasses
Point the way.

In spring
The brook beside me
Passed me by,
Beating me to the river ahead.
Its glistening rocks
Clicked together loudly then.

Noisy companion
Now rests
Quiet and dry,
Its rocks dull, grey, and still.

Fields ahead
In patterns of green and gold
Layer toward the Tetons.
But dark clouds
Rise behind me.
I turn back to the hills
And home.

Teton Valley, Idaho, 2013

Strange September

Is it time
To give up the summer's warmth
In my bones
For autumn's chill?

Each aging year
I'm more reluctant to
Face the cold of
The coming winter.

This September's sunny days
And clear blue skies
Have given way
To stormy, rain soaked nights.

The dog runs and hides
As we awake to lighting,
While thunder shakes our skies.

Compass flowers
Continue following the sun,
But the *chamisa*'s golden bloom
Is late to decorate
The flooded roadsides.

Record- breaking rains
Have blessed some with
Gifts of grass,
While others are trapped
In miles of mud.

How did our autumn world
Get so divided?

Autumn 2013

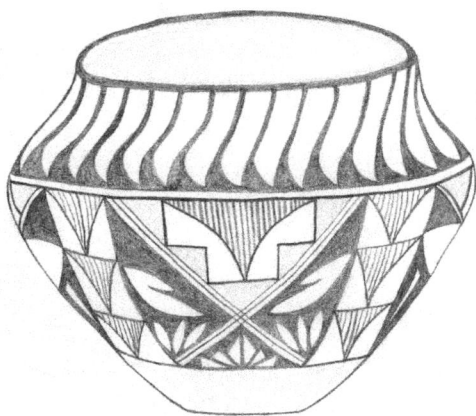

ART AND BEAUTY

The Exhibition

I entered the exhibition
And stepped into a world
Of creativity, color and texture,
A world of magic.

What seemed exquisite paintings
Were New Mexico artists' quilts,
With multi-colored palettes of
Fabrics, fibers, and stitches.

Art quilts hung against white walls,
Displaying skills and talents
I had never imagined possible.

Walking from one to another,
I was amazed, uplifted
As the stitches intertwined
Into elaborate shapes and patterns.
I felt the joy of the artists
As their stories unfolded.

What had begun
A cold, difficult day
Was now a gift,
A day to treasure.

Exhibition of Fiber Art, Rotunda Art Gallery, Santa Fe,
New Mexico, April 2013

Flame

Flame can bring destruction
Loss and pain.
Yet, when it came to us
In the dark times
We learned to soothe,
And tame it
To guide, warm and feed us.

Through the centuries
Some learned
To control it more,
To fire a pot
Prepared of
Clay and ash
From Mother Earth
And mold it
To a useful shape.

Down through the years
Our families taught us
How to use the flame
And now we create
Forms of special beauty
That will live for generations.

In honor of all Pueblo Potters of New Mexico, May 2013

Love Dolls

Side by side
They hang against the wall
Smiling at me.
Smoke-tanned buckskin
Blackfeet Love Dolls

Their ribbon sashes
Of turquoise, yellow
Orange, red and brown
Hang neatly from their waists.

Tiny colored beads for eyes,
Smiling mouths
And the trim around
Their cookie-cutter shapes.

Made as wedding gifts
They become toys for
Children later born.
Bringing harmony and love
To their lives as well.

This treasured couple
Was made for me
By the Blackfeet beader
I met at Indian Market
One day in Santa Fe.

43

Love Dolls by Jackie Parsons, Blackfeet Nation

The Basket Weaver

Gathering sumac
Along the river to
Strip, split, soak and dye,
She gives a prayer
Before beginning.

Devoted to her task
Of shaping beauty from tradition,
Her coiled basket grows
Each day from dawn to dusk.

Strong, sturdy fingers
Tightly weaving
For more than forty years.
Are now tired and aching.

She holds the basket
In a curve,
And prays for energy
Before the fire.

Preserver of the old ways
Creator of the new,
Reviver of ceremonial baskets
And modern storyteller.

Challenger of taboos
To preserve Navajo history
With bold designs and figures
Of legends and beliefs.

Many times honored and awarded
Mary is the Navajo matriarch
Of the basket world.

In honor of Navajo basket weaver Mary Black

To Be Like Mary

Full of love and wonder
For each flower, tree,
Insect, bird and beast
That welcomes her.
Her awe of God's creations
Begins with the dawn.

Each hour of her day
Brings a gift as she walks
Forest trails, a beach, or rocky shore.

Comfort and peace
Settle on her shoulders
As she watch the lives
Of mushrooms, egrets, daisies,
And finds grace
In each leaf, rock, and creature.

She seeks understanding
Of science, history, religion
From owls and vultures,
And the changing seasons.

With golden language
She observes each living thing
In ponds and puddles
And find rebirth
In the snake's shedding skin.

From rain
She learns compassion
For the world's
Suffering and pain.

Mary,
To be so full of love
For all creatures,
And so positive
Of kindness
In our world
Is to be envied.

For Mary Oliver whose poems are companions. July 2013.

The Potter

Carved or etched
Horse, frog, child
Or sacred serpent.
Simple designs of wit
And celebration
Gird stone-polished pots
Of smooth brown-fired clay.

Tradition is her base
To shape, form and fire,
But today's world
And her own life
Inspire these new designs.

The shy Santa Clara child
Sheltered in the portal's shade
Where she began'
Flanked by family
Steeped in tradition

Now with recognition
And awards bestowed,
She has stepped
Into her mature center
Of exceptional creativity.

Our hands delight
To the touch of ancient shapes
Our eyes smile
At the joyful designs
And we warm to the clay gifts
She brings us.

In honor of Jody Naranjo,
Santa Clara potter, Summer 2013

The Writer

Like the finest web
Glistening with pearls of dew
Shining in the early sun,
He weaves his words
In poetic threads
Connecting lives
Through time,
Generations.

People of history and fiction
Touch or pass each other by.
As his tale unfolds
Back and forth
Through the centuries.

Language full and flowing,
Flowering
Expands our imagination
While we share the telling.

His words cast a magic spell
Capturing us in his web of pages.
Till we are lost,
Trapped in his complex world
Of interwoven lives.

The cadence of a plane propeller,
A horse-drawn carriage,
A drum or bird song,
Words march along
In steady beat,
A rhythmic motion.

So many eloquent phrases
Expressed never before
To be remembered after.
But will I?

In honor of Colum McCann's novel <u>Transatlantic</u>

The Beaders

Patience, skill
Artistry acquired,
Children learn from
Mothers and grandmothers,
Devoted to their work.

Creating dolls
With hides, quills, beads and shells
Of intricate designs,
Each day they sew
From dawn to dusk.

Three generations
Gather at the table
Working together
With love and knowledge
Of their people.

Each doll unique,
Dignified, a work of art,
Resplendent in its regalia.
A document of tradition,
A teacher of a tribal story.

With tiny stitches
An image comes to life.
A chief or warrior,
Woman or child,
We would have seen
At ceremonies long past.

*In honor of Joyce Growing Thunder, daughter Juanita, and
granddaughter Jessa Rae, Assiniboine/Sioux, National
Museum of the American Indian, Autumn 2013*

Window Dressing

Cityscape reflections
Overlay giant walls of glass
Separating us
From enticing mannequins
Urging us to come inside.

Statements of luxury,
Their stylish clothes
And stilted poses
Echo the sharp lines
Of claustrophobic skyscrapers
Rising to the sky.

Signs and city lights,
Office windows,
Passersby
Make surreal patterns
Of black and white
Which flow across the glass.

Light and forms
Merge and fuse
With shop displays
Of jewels and clothes,
Alluring samples
 Of the world of fashion.

All is fragmented,
Distorted,
And finalized
Into bold works of art,
Stunning statements
Made with a camera's lens.

*In honor of photographer Lee Friedlander and his show
"Mannequin" at the Andrew Smith Gallery, Santa Fe,
October 2013*

Georgia's Lake

"It is really lovely," she wrote,
Escaping to her shanty
To paint autumn's gold and brown
Or lush shades of summer green.
"Leaves are like rare flowers."

Old trees are seen in changing moods,
The sensuality of summer blooms unfolds.
Petunia, Jimson, Calla Lily, Morning Glory
Jack-in-the-Pulpit
Are enlarged to graceful abstraction.

Silent, empty barns,
Reminders of her childhood,
Are made of geometric shapes
In brooding colors.
Their small, blank windows unrevealing,
Precursors of adobe homes.

Apple orchards,
Mountain walks
Her corn garden
And lakeside views
Express her love of nature
Long before New Mexico.

*In honor of the Lake George paintings of Georgia O'Keeffe
seen at the Georgia O'Keeffe Museum, Autumn 2013.*

Listening to Country

Hard Rock is mostly painful noise
Which smothers words and blurs.
Country's words ring clear,
And are pleasing to my ear.

In troubadour tradition
Country singers
Write lyrics
Of life, injustice,
Love, loss, and fears
Written as they travel
On the road,
True balladeers.

I have heard their storytelling songs
Down through so many years.
Melodic or profound,
There are lyrics that can move me
As much as any famous poets' lines.

In honor of the legends of country music, singing poets
of my generation, November 2013

HISTORY LESSONS

Hawa Mahal

Shaped like Krishna's crown
Made of sandstone
Red and pink
My Palace of the Winds
Is now a tourist treasure

Many years ago
It gave me shelter
To observe Purdah
While I watched
Jaipur's life go by below.

Unseen by those below
I walked the inside slopes
Of my royal place
To look through
Small windows of delicate design
At the people and processions
Passing by.

My days were spent
Watching children, merchants,
Beggars and rich men,
Or strolling through
Our spacious courtyards
Behind this intricate façade.

Maharaja Sawai Pratap Singh built the Palace of the Winds in 1799.

Son of War

What Have You Done?
Son of war,
Molded for battle.
Taught to kill and hate,
To fight the enemy
Not be its helpful mate.

Still
How could you kill
Children and families
In their sleep?

The demons of your mind
Have led you
To despair,
And all are gone.

Like oil and water.
Peace-maker and
Trained killer
Cannot blend.
Some of you
Will never mend.

Do we ask too much
Of those
Whose repeated tours
Drain them
Of all humanity?

Yes.
And we now pay the price
Of creating you,
Unable to distinguish
Friend from foe.

We must not only mourn
Those lost lives,
But when you cross the line
We are all in peril.

March 2012, Marine Corps sniper, Iraq

The Sash

Sheltered under glass
The brilliant sash glows
Between the dull brown ancient pots.
This most treasured relic,
Symbol of wealth and status,
Holds us in its spell.

One thousand parrot feathers,
Blue and orange,
Sewn tightly
Around strands of yucca,
Centuries ago,
Still shimmer in the light.

Though found in local ruins,
The sash seems freshly made.
Only the hide suggests its age.
Its feathers of Macaw,
Brought north in trade,
Remain undimmed by time.

Why was this perfect piece
Of power and beauty made?
A spoil of war passed down to son?
A gift to priest, king or queen?
What honor did it bring?
What tradition did it mean?

*This Macaw Feather Sash, dated to 1150 A.D. is the
centerpiece of the Pre-Colombian collection at the Edge
of the Cedars State Park Museum in Blanding, Utah.*

Sandy Hook

<u>December 14, 2012</u>

She held his hand
Excited for a new school day.
They did not say goodbye.

Instead of fun,
His teacher shooed them
Into a corner like a mother hen.
She said she loved them,
And promised the good guys
Would come
To stop the one who had the gun.

Later, his parents came,
Both crying hard,
To hold him tight
And tell him,
His sister, one of twenty-six,
Would not be home tonight,
Never again to give them joy and light.

<u>October 2013</u>

While autumn leaves are falling,
Bulldozers arrive.
All material memories
To be erased,
Pulverized to dust.
No souvenirs left behind
For the first anniversary
Of a town unhealed.

Decided by vote, at agonizing meetings,
There will be no official ceremony.
Most decided for destruction,
Unable to imagine child, teacher
Or parent returning there.
In a few years a new school will
Welcome the next generation.

The Lost Boys

We are the Lost Boys
Thousands of us,
Children lost in time.
We ran from childhood,
Families left behind,
From the cleansing of Sudan.

For years we traveled
Walked a thousand miles
Fleeing death
Crying for our mothers,
Our homes.

We walked shoeless
Across desert lands
Of cruel sun and dust,
Crossing a wide river
Where many drowned
And bodies floated
Past us in the current.

Without water, food or comfort,
We ran to foreign lands.
Unwelcome in Ethiopia,
A camp in Kenya,
And finally a metal bird
Freed us to fly to America.

Before 9/11 we came
To Kansas, Nebraska,
Illinois, Arizona.
Rescued, to start

A strange new life
In complicated cities.

What was real or fantasy?
We could not tell.
We who died for water
In the desert
Saw toilets, sinks, and stoves,
Now sat by pools and fountains.

For all it has been struggle
Some succeeding
More than others
Whose lives here
Have met obstacles
Along the way.

Abraham fulfilled his dream
To minister and speak of faith.
Now Episcopal Bishop
In newly independent
South Sudan.

Joseph has not met
His childhood dream
To become a doctor,
That traveled with him
To America.

Becoming citizens
In our adopted land,
Many of us now have
Children of our own.

Others speak by Internet
To awe-struck mothers
Who thought them dead,
And pray for reunions
In their homeland.

What has happened
To children left behind?
Are they all gone?
Or did they survive
To return home in time?

We are the Lost Boys
Whose stories
Are of suffering, fear and hunger.
Whom Abraham says
"…were lost, but not to God."

*In memory of thousands of children fleeing the ethnic
cleansing in the Sudan in 2001.*

Fire Flash

They are gone to ash.
Nineteen families
Forever changed
Will struggle to remain.

Their hearts and souls
Have left each one,
Caught in sudden tragedy
Only nature can bestow.

We cannot ponder
Their painful ends
As fire trapped them
In its deathly grip.

With our prayers
And half-masted flags,
We show our honor
For their sacrifice.

We must accept
Their answer to Death's call
With their strength and bravery
"...this day on the line."

For the Granite Mountain Hot Shot Firemen of Prescott
Arizona, July, 2013

Mandela

From every corner,
Thousands of odes,
Songs of praise
And prayers
Fill the air for you
And I wish to add my voice.

Madiba
We all have said goodbye
So many times
Beginning with your
Prison road.
We never felt
It was the end.
Until now at ninety-five
Our friend.

For twenty-seven years
An eight by eight cell,
A small window's
Distant mountain
Kept hope alive for you.

Generations have grown up
In your protective shadow
You urged us to be strong
Against apartheid,
To be patient,
To do our duty.

Free at last,
You shook many hands
And taught forgiveness.
We welcomed you back
To be our first black leader.
Then you walked away from power,

The years have passed.
You taught us well.
A role model like no other,
Your duty's done.
Your life has changed the world.
Now you can rest for eternity.

While you have been leaving
We have been preparing
To be without you.
Yet did not imagine
The depth of loss
The world would feel.

December 2013

National Treasure

Kept safe in its cardboard nest,
A museum treasure
Too fragile to put to the test.
The simple design
A telephone of
Small gourds connected
By a long cotton twine
Twelve hundred years ago.

As children we loved
Our tin can and string
Communicators.
Not knowing an inventor
In Peru's Rio Moche valley
Made one so long ago.

Before the Incas ruled,
His sophisticated world
Had artisans, metalworkers
And engineers, whose canals
Transformed dry deserts
To fertile lands.

What caused
This sound transmitter
To be invented?
Perhaps a courtier or servant,
Forbidden to speak
Directly to his master or high priest,
Sent messages unseen
From room to room.

This first known telephone is the only one ever found. It is in the National Museum of the American Indian storage facility in Maryland.

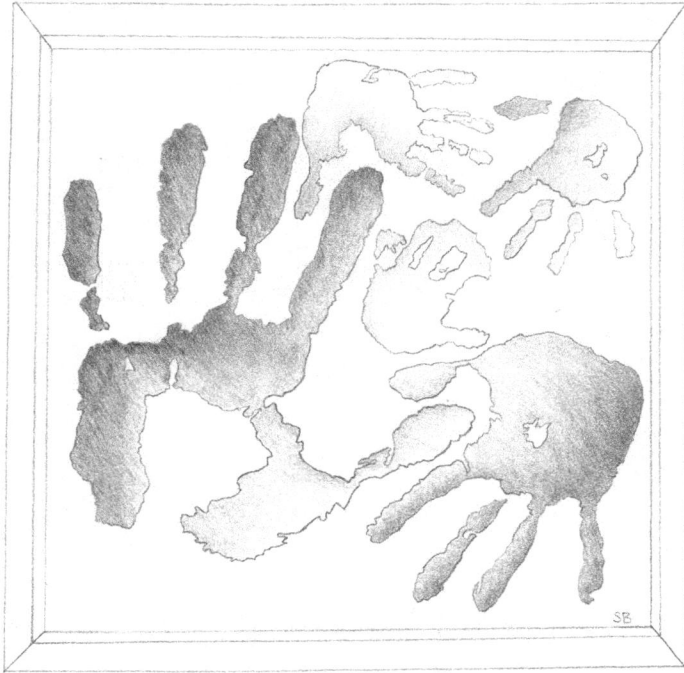

FAMILY AND FRIENDS

"Fallen Feather"

Your painting "Fallen Feather,"
Masked spirit man,
Guards the entry to our home.
We came to Santa Fe
Like you, to change direction and
Seek inspiration from this ancient land.

Your copper circle of life,
Embedded in a petroglyph story
Graces another wall.
With these treasures
You are always with us.

We celebrate your life
And share special memories
With all who are your family,
Recall your love of life,
Strong laugh, and stinging wit.

Do all know your many talents,
Stone carver, potter, painter?
Travel well in the years ahead
You are not alone,
One day we will be with you.

For now we remember you
The way you were,
Courageous, feisty woman
At home, and smiling in the sun
On your favorite beach.

Cancer could not defeat you
First time round.
It took the second blow
To wear you down.

In memory of artist and friend Ellen Peebler, May 2011

Night Lights

Flying

Moving,
Or suspended
Above an unseen earth?
Darkness wraps around the windows.
Engine noise the only way
To be sure we are heading west.

A sudden glimmer.
Scattered tiny lights below,
Then small clusters blossom
Until we are approaching
A vast grid of lights
Leading us home.

On a Desert Road

Twilight's murky haze of grey
Fades to black,
As in a theatre
When the lights dim
And we sit soundless,
Expectant,
Waiting for the curtain-rise.

Our headlights mark the road ahead,
Leading us into the night.
A glint of starlight on phone lines
Our only guide to the horizon,
Where stars are mimicked by
Earth-bound twinkling lights.

The Train

Pittsburgh to Boston,
Boarding at midnight.
My father waves good-bye
As I set out on the first adventure
Of my college years.

Lights flash briefly as we
Fly past small town stations
And lonely farms.
I am rocked to sleep
In my narrow bunk.

Penn Station.
I wake to voices,
And metal-screeching wheels,
As we are disconnected,
Then re-coupled
To a north bound train.

For four years
The adventure
And anticipation
Of this solo journey
Never dims
As I move from campus
To home
And back again.

December memories, 2011

Celebrating Joan

A black velvet mantle,
Night spreads out below,
Embroidered with jewels
Of twinkling lights
As our plane descends to earth.

Joan has brought us back,
Family, friends and colleagues,
To embrace, laugh, and cry
While we celebrate
Her rich, giving life
As wife, mother, friend,
Quiet leader and guide.

The sun and memories
 Of her joyful spirit warm us.
We recall Joan's special gifts,
Her hearty laugh,
And love of life
On this day of peace.

January 12, 2012

Friendship

A bond of friendship
Glued through time
Randy, John
Gerard, Tom.
Men with years
Of caring work
In music, arts, business,
Government careers.
But still boys at heart.

This foursome
Is proof
The whole can be
Greater than its parts.

Lunch traditions,
Weekly phone calls,
Opera tailgates,
Wove them together
Into a tapestry of
Fun times and sharing,
While supporting and serving
Our community
With skills and talents
Unsurpassed.

Randy suddenly is gone.
But his memory
Will keep the foursome
Greater than the sum
Of each one.

The glue
They forged together
Will stay strong forever.

In memory of Randy Forrester, August 2012

Lifting Weights

Mother and Grandmother
Working hard,
Lifting, kneeling,
Scrubbing, polishing,
Washing, ironing
To keep our world safe and clean.

Down through their aging years,
Their solid arms began to change,
Skin sagging from muscle and bone
As if pulled away by gravity.

Their way,
My path was not to be,
Not for me.
Lifting weights would be the answer.
My arms would remain smooth and firm.

Yet in spite of all,
My mirror twin
Shows aging muscles
Stretching beneath my sagging skin.

Autumn, 2012

Show Girl

You are the only one I know
To sing into her eighties
With a show.
Mike-less, you carried on,
Celebrating life in joyful song.

You showed your killer comic gift
When you sang about a lift,
Then, my insides nearly split.

And your Memory song
Was the funniest of all.
I laughed until I cried.
Of laughter, I might have died.
Yet now, not one word can I recall.

Your show was such a blast.
It went by much too fast.
Once again you gave your all.
We salute you with raised glass
For years of friendship
Now and past.

For Sue Lovitz, 2012

The Rocking Chair

A moonless night
With stars so bright
Outside her window.

Brothers sleeping now,
Soccer game exhaustion.
But Maggie remains awake
Crying for her mother.

Sitting tight together
In the rocking chair
Her warmth spreads
Along my side.

We whisper in the dark,
Staring at the night light's glow,
Until her sturdy small being
Unwinds, curls up and stills
As we rock on.

Drooping with fatigue
From our grandchildren's day
I am slowly fading away.

Once in bed
She seems sound asleep.
I try to creep away.

At the door's small creak
Up pops her head.
Cries for Mommy
Bring us back,
Snugly side by side
In the rocking chair.

Idaho summer 2013

Wartime Memories

Streetlights off.
The wallpaper roses
And white woodwork
Of my room
Fade in the darkness.

My father pulls
Blackout shades
Down my windows
And kisses me goodnight.

A Pittsburgh wartime night,
City of steel,
Feared to be a target.

Ten and six
At Pearl Harbor time,
Paul and I
Learn to do our share.

Stomping cans
On the basement floor,
Sticking small stamps
On war bond savings books.

Food rationing
Means chicken, sausage, hams
From our cousin's farm.

Mom kneads a bag of Oleo,
Mixing a white waxy blob
With a pill of orange dye
To turn it butter yellow.

Paul and I stare at
The cow's tongue
Garlanded with boiled potatoes.
We must eat dinner
To earn the apple pie.

Dad takes his turn
At night patrol
When not making
House calls.

Uncle Paul comes home,
Dressed in blue,
A handsome Navy Captain
With his new wife.
I wear his gold-braid trimmed hat.

A marine on Guam,
Cousin Guy returns
Bringing us a treasure bag,
Full of Cowry shells.

Stories of others
Who don't return
Are whispered in other rooms.

As the years of wartime summers
Continue on,
Our Victory Garden
Takes over the back yard.

Grandma bakes pies and bread,
Cans beans and cabbage,
Stews tomatoes,
While Mom plays
Patriotic songs on her piano.

We are protected
From our parents fears
And war's hardships.
Our childhood stays safe.

Later on, we learn
We were the lucky ones.

Recalling childhood memories of World War II.

CODA

Coda Number Four

Now I'm ending
Book number four,
Should I once again
Say "Never more"?

Who knows
Through eyes,
Ears and nose,
What theme
May come my way
To begin anew
Any day?

Writing causes such an itch
It can't be turned off
Just with a switch.
At times
It sleeps or hides away
When life decisions
Get in the way.

It is best to say
"Goodbye" just for now.
Like the sleeping bear
I'll wake one dawn
The itch still there,
It's never gone.

Autumn, 2013

Readers Guide

Landscape: I wrote the poem *Linemen* after watching the big power lines stretching along the highway on one of our road trips in the Southwest. Can you think of other man-made objects in your landscape or cityscape that seem to have human characteristics?

Wild and Tame: Not many of us have the opportunity to experience the release of a recovered wild bird or animal. In my poem *Osprey*, I hope I have related how lucky I felt to witness the release of this wild bird. Have you ever had an occasion to appreciate the work of those dedicated to caring for birds and animals, wild or domestic?

Seasons: The changing seasons are important to many of us, even if we are city dwellers. I believe a sudden change in weather in a particular season can affect our mood. At the end of *Summer Walk*, dark clouds threaten a peaceful summer afternoon. I suddenly felt uncomfortable and turn back to go home. Does a change of season or weather ever affect your mood?

Art and Beauty: This is the first time I have devoted a section of a book of poetry to my thoughts about art and beauty. I have included the poem *Listening to Country* in this section because I personally feel country music singers

deserve to be considered artists as much as a
painter, writer or opera singer. Do you agree or
disagree?

History Lessons: Have you ever read an
article about an exotic, ancient place that you
realize you will probably never visit, but your
imagination is sparked? You may imagine what
it might have been like to live there long ago.
My poem *Hawa Mahal* is about one of my
imaginative experiences. Think about your own
imaginative experiences, perhaps the result
of reading, taking a trip, or meeting someone
unusual.

Family and Friends: The poem *Night Lights*
is meant to describe my feelings about lights
in the darkness when I was leaving or coming
home. When we are traveling at night, lights
may be comforting, or sometimes a bit scary.
Have you had personal experiences when lights
in the darkness have had an effect on you?

www.ingramcontent.com/pod-product-compliance
Lightning Source LLC
La Vergne TN
LVHW091229080426
835509LV00009B/1219